PIANO • VOCAL • GUITAR

TOP ▶ REQUESTED
Classic
SHEET MUSIC

20 ROCK MASTERPIECES ARRANGED FOR PIANO AND VOICE

Contents

Produced by
Alfred Music
P.O. Box 10003
Van Nuys, CA 91410-0003
alfred.com

Printed in USA.

ISBN-10: 0-7390-9844-6
ISBN-13: 978-0-7390-9844-8

Cover photo: © Shutterstock.com / Anna Omelchenko

 Alfred Cares. Contents printed on 100% recycled paper.

ALL MY LOVE

Words and Music by
JOHN PAUL JONES and ROBERT PLANT

Moderately (♩ = 92)

1. Should I fall out of love, my fire in the light,___

you now.   All of my love,___   all of my love,___   oh,

To Coda ⊕ |1. |2.

all of my love___   to   you now.   you, child.

(Guitar)

BEHIND BLUE EYES

Words and Music by
PETER TOWNSHEND

*Harmonies sung 2nd time.

14

Lyrics:
fool.__

And if I swal - low an - y - thing e -

vil, put your fin - ger down__ my throat. And if I shiv - er, please give me a

blan - ket. Keep me warm,___ let me wear your coat.___

Chords: Bm A E Bm A E | Bm G D Bm A D | Bm A E Bm | A E Bm A B

BRIDGE OVER TROUBLED WATER

Words and Music by
PAUL SIMON

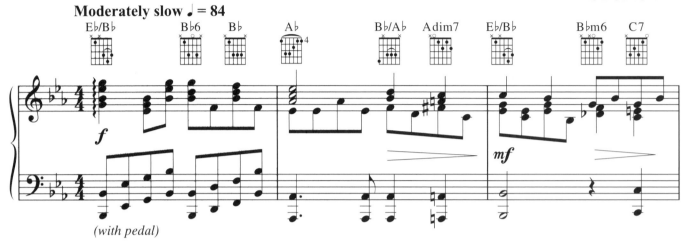

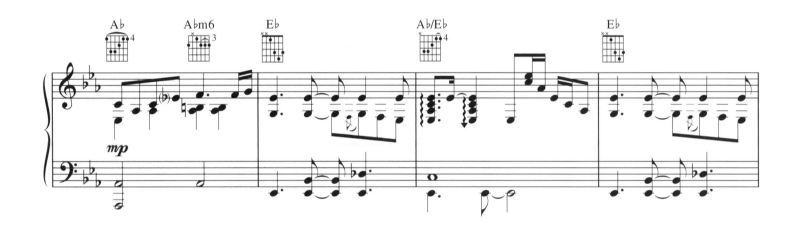

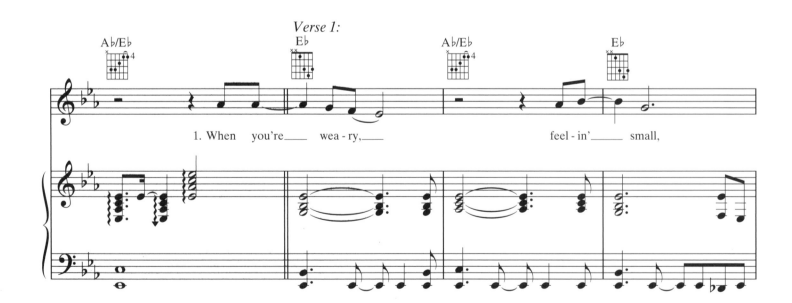

1. When you're___ wea - ry,___ feel - in'___ small,

DON'T STOP BELIEVIN'

Words and Music by
JONATHAN CAIN, NEAL SCHON
and STEVE PERRY

Don't Stop Believin' - 4 - 1

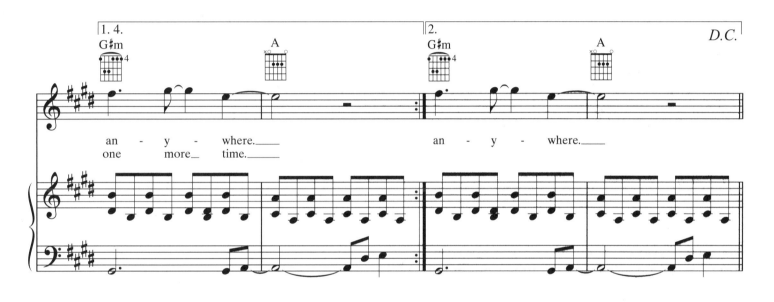

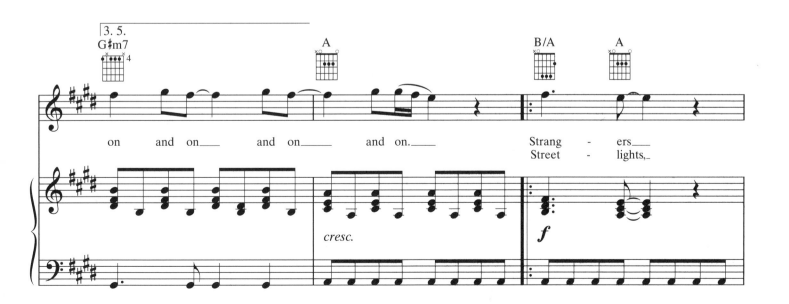

FAITHFULLY

Words and Music by
JONATHAN CAIN

E   B

Wheels go 'round_ and 'round,___ you're on my mind.
We all need___ the clowns___ to make us smile.

Rest - less hearts   sleep a -
Through space and time,   al - ways an -

G#m   E

lone to - night,___   send - in' all___ my love___ a - long the
oth - er___ show.___   Won - d'ring where___ I am,___ lost with -

B/F#   F#   E   G#m

wire._____   They say that the road ain't no___ place to start a fam-
out   you.___   And be - in' a - part ain't eas - y   on this love

faith - ful - ly._____

2. Cir - cus

Oh,_____ oh,_____

oh._____

I SAW HER STANDING THERE

Words and Music by
JOHN LENNON and PAUL McCARTNEY

Fast rock ♩ = 160

1. Well, she was just___

Verses 1 & 2:

___ sev - en - teen,___ and you know what I mean.___
looked at me___ and I, I___ could see

___ And the way she looked was way be - yond com - pare.___
that be - fore too long I___ fell in love_ with her.___

I Saw Her Standing There - 6 - 1

Guitar solo:

IMAGINE

Words and Music by
JOHN LENNON

Moderately slow ♩ = 75

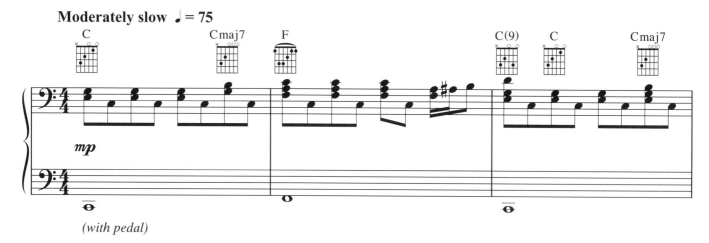

mp

(with pedal)

Verse 1:

1. Im-ag-ine there's   no heav-en.____

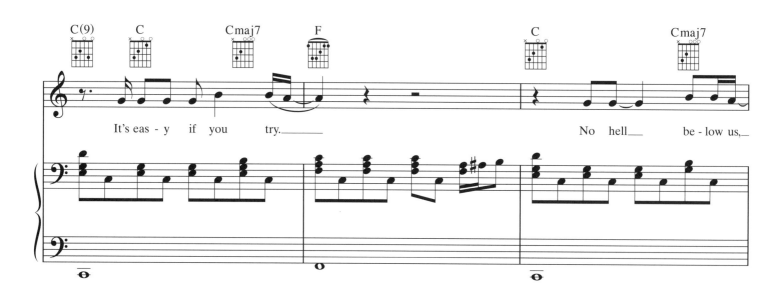

It's eas-y if you   try._____   No hell____   be-low us,

Imagine - 4 - 1

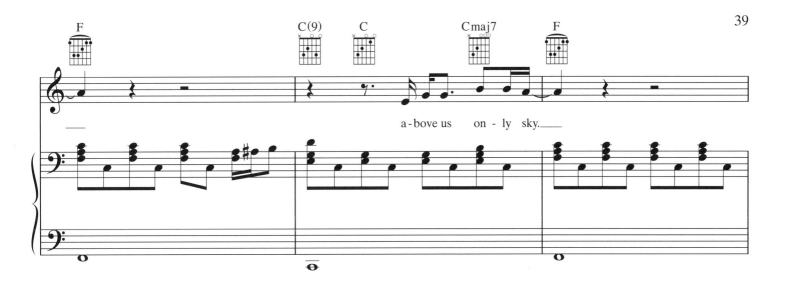

a - bove us   on - ly sky.___

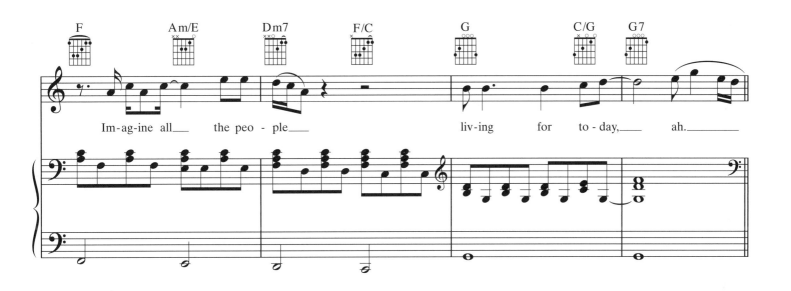

Im - ag - ine all___ the peo - ple___   liv - ing   for   to - day,___   ah.___

Verse 2: (Sing 2nd time only)

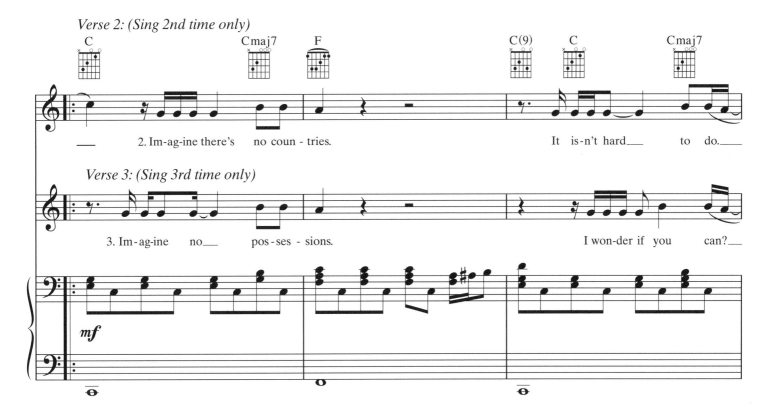

___   2. Im-ag-ine there's   no coun - tries.   It is-n't hard___   to do.___

Verse 3: (Sing 3rd time only)

3. Im-ag-ine   no___   pos-ses - sions.   I won-der if you   can?___

LIVE AND LET DIE

Words and Music by
PAUL McCARTNEY and LINDA McCARTNEY

Slowly (♩ = 60)

When you were young and your heart was an o-pen book,___
(2nd time, instrumental till _____ *)*

You used to say live and let live. (You know you did, you know you did, you know you

did.___) But if this ev-er-chang-ing world in which we live in makes you

Live and Let Die - 4 - 1

C 9
*8va lower ad lib. till**

What does it mat-ter to ya,

when you got a job to do___ you got-ta   do it well.___   You got-ta

give the oth - er fel - low hell!

D.C. al Coda

Coda

BIG YELLOW TAXI

Words and Music by
JONI MITCHELL

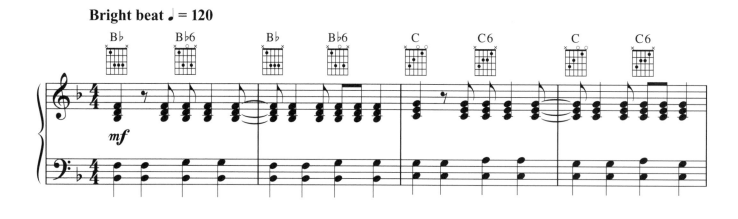

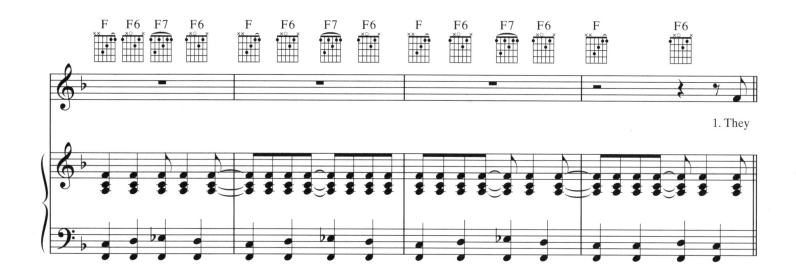

1. They

Verse:

paved par-a-dise   and   put   up   a   park-ing   lot___
took   all   the   trees   and   put   them   in   a   tree   mu-se-um,
3. Hey,   farm-er,   farm-er,   put   a-way   that   D.   D.   T.____   now.
4. Late   last___   night,   I   heard   the___   screen_   door   slam___

Big Yellow Taxi - 3 - 1

MONEY

Words and Music by
ROGER WATERS

TRO - © 1973 (Renewed) HAMPSHIRE HOUSE PUBLISHING CORP., New York, N.Y.

sax. solo ad lib.

PLAY THAT FUNKY MUSIC

Words and Music by
ROBERT PARISSI

Moderate funk ♩ = 108

playin' in a rock and roll band.___
changin' rock and roll - in' minds.___

I nev - er had no prob - lems,___
And things were get - tin' shak - y.___

___ yeah,
___

burn - in' down the one - night stands.___
I thought I'd have to leave it be -

hind.

And ev - 'ry - thing a - round me,___
But now it's so much bet - ter.___

Chorus:

PINBALL WIZARD

Words and Music by
PETER TOWNSHEND

Moderate rock ♩ = 126

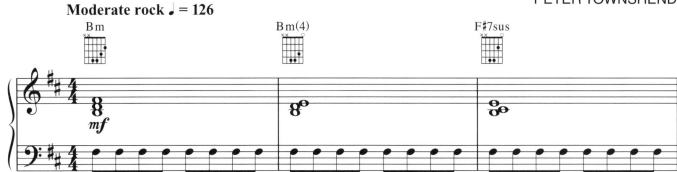

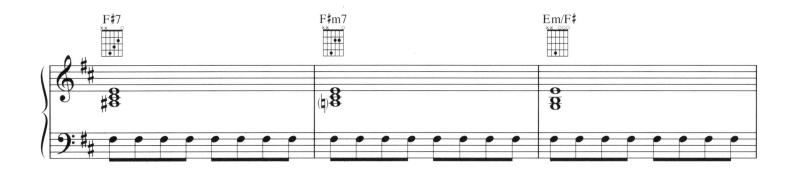

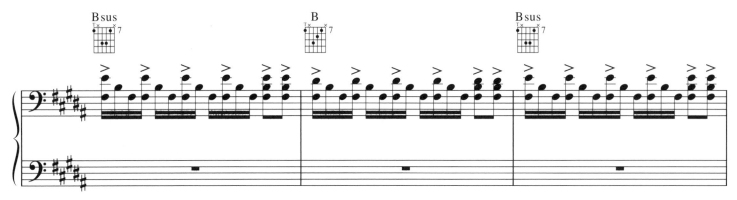

Verse 1:

Verses 2 & 3:

SATURDAY IN THE PARK

Words and Music by
ROBERT LAMM

Saturday in the Park - 7 - 1

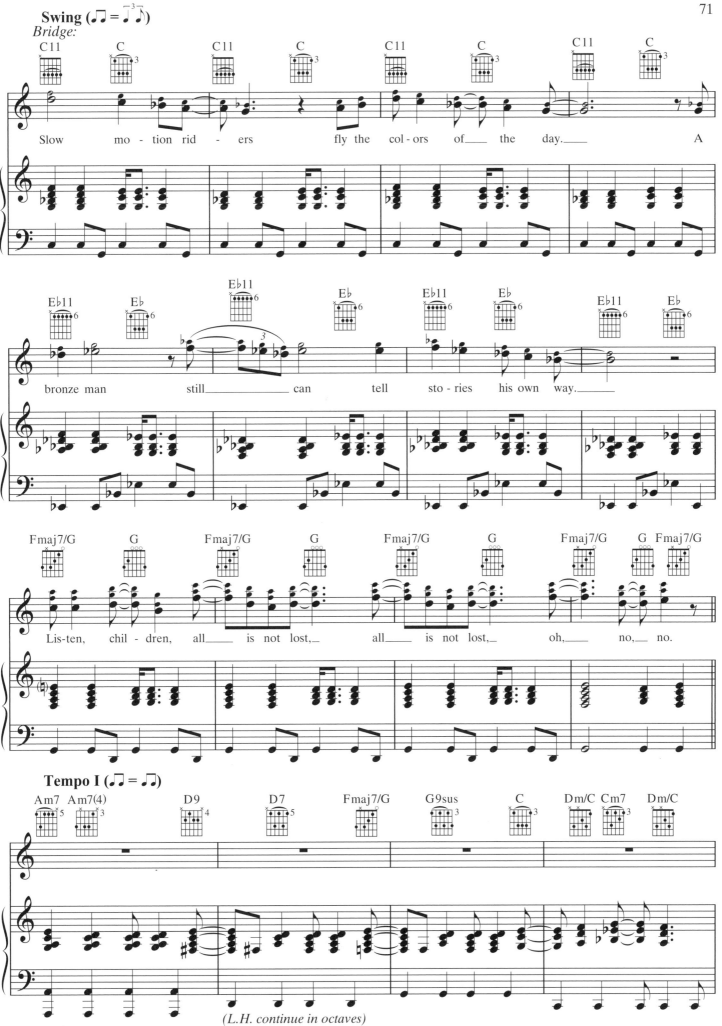

ST. STEPHEN

Words by
ROBERT HUNTER

Music by
JERRY GARCIA and PHIL LESH

Moderately slow ♩ = 63

p

accel.

Faster ♩ = 96
Verse 1:

mf

1. Saint Ste - phen with a rose, _____ in and out ___ of the gar - den he goes.

Coun - try gar - den in the wind _ and the rain; wher - ev - er he goes, _ the peo - ple all ___ com - plain.

St. Stephen - 6 - 1

Dark-ness shrugs and bids the day good-bye. Speed-ing ar-row, sharp and

nar-row, what a lot of fleet-ing mat-ters you have spurned. Sev-'ral sea-sons

with their trea-sons wrap the babe in scar-let col-ors, call it your own.

N.C.

accel.

Faster ♩ = 96

78

Verses 3 & 4:

E⁷   D2⁵   A⁵   E⁷

3. Did he doubt_ or did he try?_____ An - swers a - plen - ty in the by - and - by.
4. Saint_ Ste - phen will re - main;_____ all he's lost_ he_ shall re - gain.

1.

D⁵   N.C.

Talk a - bout your plen - ty, talk_ a - bout your ills; one man gath-ers what an-oth-er man_ spills.
Sea - shore_ washed by the suds_ and the foam, been

a tempo

Repeat ad lib. and fade

STAIRWAY TO HEAVEN

Words and Music by
JIMMY PAGE and ROBERT PLANT

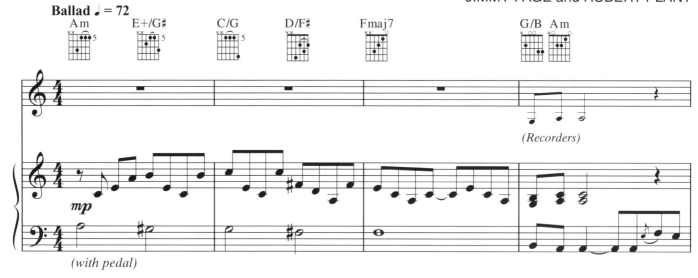

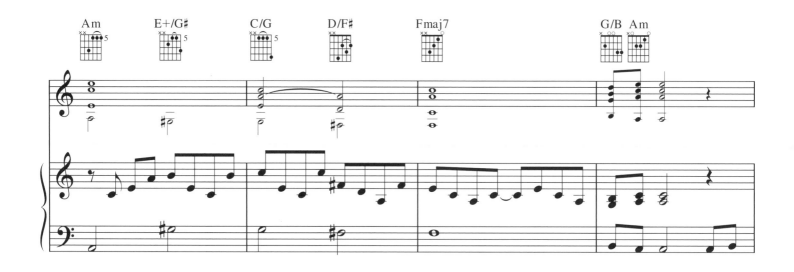

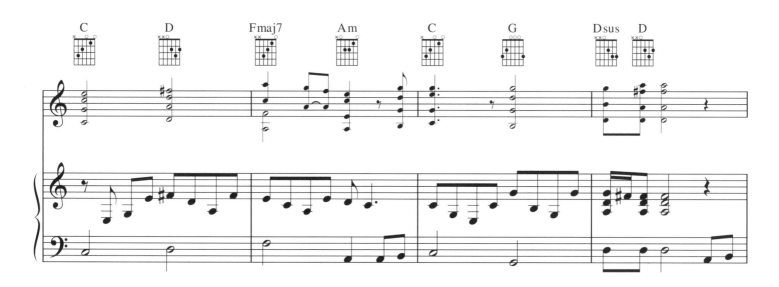

Stairway to Heaven - 12 - 1

Slightly faster

Ooo,_____ it makes me won - der.

Ooo,_____ makes me won - der._____

2. There's a

Verses 2 & 3:

feel - ing I get__ when I look to the west,__ and my spir - it is cry-ing for leav-
whis - pered that soon__ if we all call the tune,__ then the pip - er will lead us to rea-

ing. In my thoughts I have seen__ rings of smoke through the trees,___ and the
son. And a new day will dawn,_ for those who stand long,____ and the

voic - es of those who stand look - ing.
for - ests will ech - o with laugh - ter.

Ooh,____ it makes me won - der.

SPACE ODDITY

Words and Music by
DAVID BOWIE

Moderately slow ♩ = 72

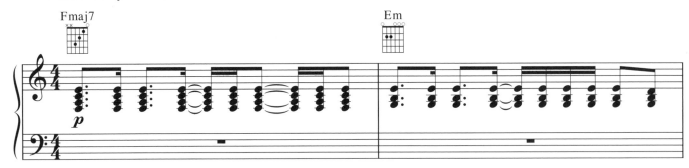

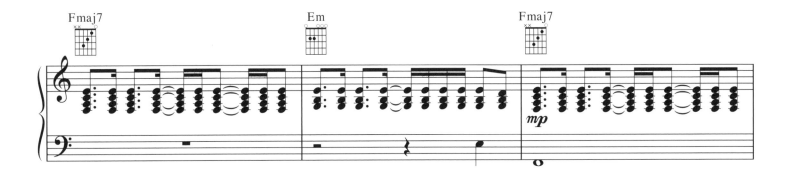

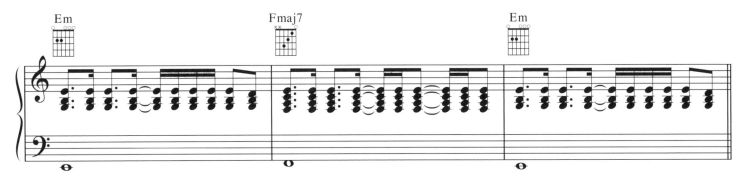

Verse:

Ground con-trol___ to Ma - jor Tom.___

Space Oddity - 7 - 1

TOM SAWYER

Words by
PYE DUBOIS and NEIL PEART

Music by
GEDDY LEE and ALEX LIFESON

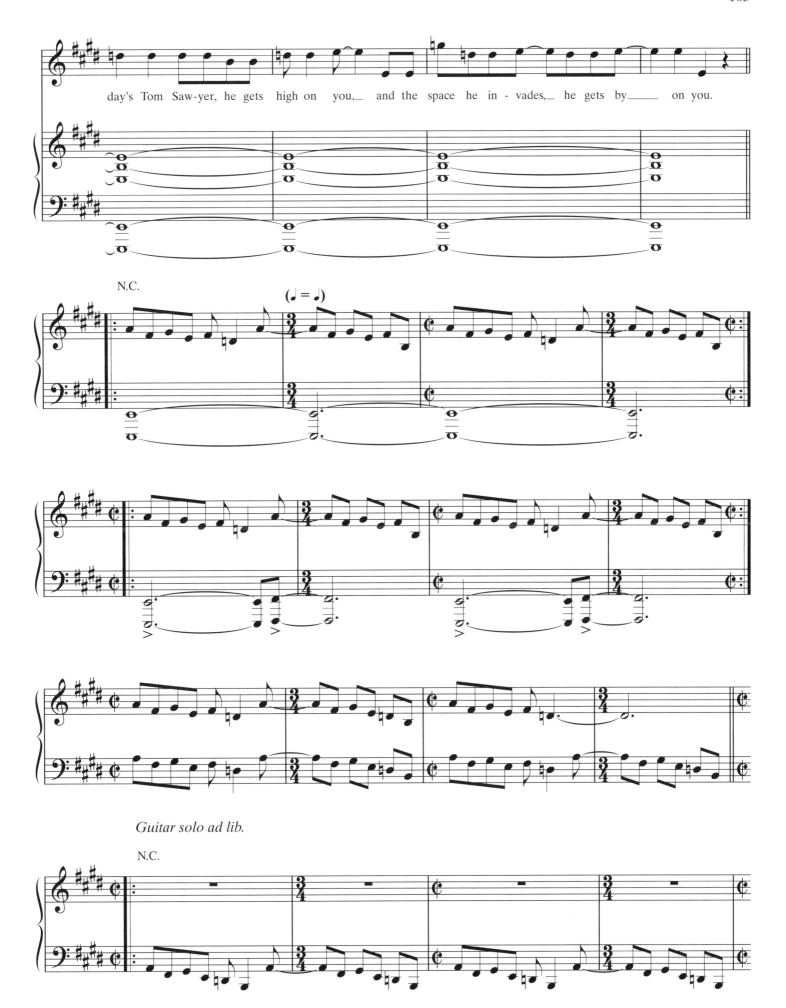

day's Tom Saw-yer, he gets high on you,__ and the space he in - vades,__ he gets by_____ on you.

Guitar solo ad lib.

N.C.

D.S. % al Coda

THUNDER ROAD

Words and Music by
BRUCE SPRINGSTEEN

Thunder Road - 10 - 1

Instrumental:

Tenor Sax.:

YOU CAN'T ALWAYS GET WHAT YOU WANT

Guitar in Open E tuning *(optional w/ Capo at 8th fret):*
⑥ = E ③ = G♯
⑤ = B ② = B
④ = E ① = E

Words and Music by
MICK JAGGER and KEITH RICHARDS

Moderately ♩ = 104

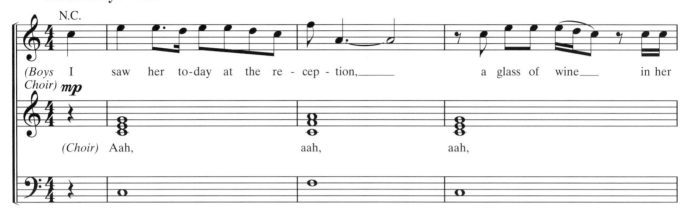

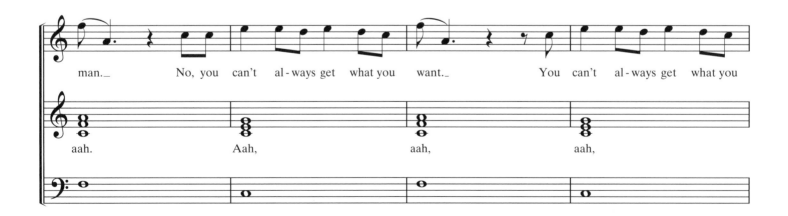

You Can't Always Get What You Want - 10 - 1

(Lead Vocal) 1. I

𝄋 *Verses 1 & 5:*

saw her to - day___ at the re - cep - - tion,
5. *See additional lyrics*

a glass of wine_____ in her hand._____ I knew_

___ she was gon - na meet her con - nec - - tion._____ At her

Verse 3:
I went down to the Chelsea drugstore
To get your prescription filled.
I was standin' in line with Mr. Jimmy.
A-man, did he look pretty ill.

Verse 4:
We decided that we would have a soda;
My favorite flavor, cherry red,
I sung my song to Mr. Jimmy.
Yeah, and he said one word to me, and that was "dead."
I said to him…
(To Chorus:)

Verse 5:
I saw her today at the reception.
In her glass was a bleeding man.
She was practiced at the art of deception.
Well, I could tell by her blood-stained hands.
Say it!
(To Chorus:)

A WHITER SHADE OF PALE

Words and Music by
KEITH REID and GARY BROOKER

A Whiter Shade of Pale - 3 - 1